Animal Sanctuaries

Kelli Hicks

rourkeeducationalmedia.com

Scan for Related Titles
and Teacher Resources

Before Reading:

Building Academic Vocabulary and Background Knowledge

Before reading a book, it is important to tap into what your child or students already know about the topic. This will help them develop their vocabulary, increase their reading comprehension, and make connections across the curriculum.

1. Look at the cover of the book. What will this book be about?
2. What do you already know about the topic?
3. Let's study the Table of Contents. What will you learn about in the book's chapters?
4. What would you like to learn about this topic? Do you think you might learn about it from this book? Why or why not?
5. Use a reading journal to write about your knowledge of this topic. Record what you already know about the topic and what you hope to learn about the topic.
6. Read the book.
7. In your reading journal, record what you learned about the topic and your response to the book.
8. After reading the book complete the activities below.

Content Area Vocabulary
Read the list. What do these words mean?

carnivorous
enclosures
exhibit
exotic
habitat
neglected
protected
rehabilitated
sanctuary
species
unique

After Reading:

Comprehension and Extension Activity

After reading the book, work on the following questions with your child or students in order to check their level of reading comprehension and content mastery.

1. Why are yearly inspections important to have at sanctuaries? (Asking questions)
2. Why do people want exotic animals as pets? (Summarize)
3. Can the animals at a sanctuary be released back into their wild, natural habitat? Explain. (Inferring)
4. Have you seen animals used in the entertainment industry? Where? How did it make you feel? (Text to self connection)
5. Do you think a sanctuary takes in all types of animals or a single type of animal? Explain. (Asking questions)

Extension Activity

Hidden sanctuaries. Research your state for animal sanctuaries. You may be surprised at what you find! What kind of sanctuary is it? How far is it from your town? What are some ways you can help? Create a poster that informs your school or the community about the sanctuary and ways they can help. Hang the poster up in the hallway at school or your local library.

Table of Contents

Chapter 1

Living Wild

When you think of lions and tigers in the wild, what do you see? Do you picture a sweeping savannah with long swaying grass or an African desert with hot sands and dry underbrush? Animals in the wild live in a **habitat** that provides them with a home, water, and food.

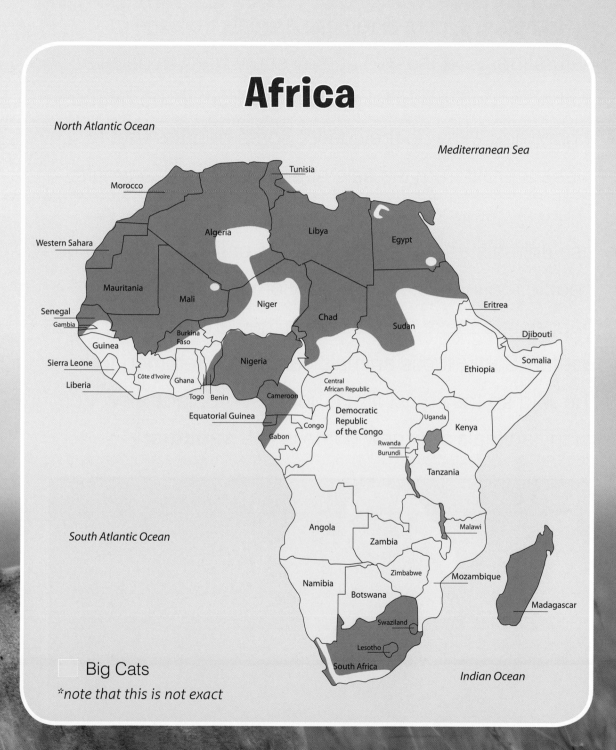

Africa

North Atlantic Ocean

Mediterranean Sea

Tunisia
Morocco
Western Sahara
Algeria
Libya
Egypt
Mauritania
Mali
Niger
Chad
Sudan
Eritrea
Djibouti
Somalia
Senegal
Gambia
Guinea
Burkina Faso
Sierra Leone
Côte d'Ivoire
Ghana
Nigeria
Cameroon
Central African Republic
Ethiopia
Liberia
Togo
Benin
Equatorial Guinea
Gabon
Congo
Democratic Republic of the Congo
Uganda
Kenya
Rwanda
Burundi
Tanzania
Angola
Zambia
Malawi
Namibia
Zimbabwe
Mozambique
Madagascar
Botswana
Swaziland
Lesotho
South Africa

South Atlantic Ocean

Indian Ocean

☐ Big Cats

note that this is not exact

Sometimes, people remove animals from their natural home in the wild. It may seem hard to believe that someone would take an animal from its home, but it happens. Why do they do it? Some people want to make a profit from the sale of **exotic**, or wild, animals. There is demand from the entertainment industry to use animals as stars in movies, TV, or live shows. Some people are interested in a fancy or **unique** pet. What happens to these animals when they are no longer useful? Sadly, these animals can not be returned to the wild so they must find a home someplace else. For many animals their new home is in a **sanctuary**.

Animals taken from their natural habitat are often used as entertainment at the expense of their happiness and ability to thrive in an unknown world.

FURRY FACT

What is a Poacher? A poacher is an individual that illegally takes an animal out of its home or kills an animal for its skin, tusks, or other body parts. Poachers are motivated by money and have contributed to a dramatic decline in the population of many animals, including African elephants.

African elephant

Chapter 2
Finding Sanctuary

An animal sanctuary is a **protected** home. It is a place where animals go to be cared for and to have a safe environment to live out their lives. A sanctuary provides all the care an animal needs to have the best life possible.

Unfortunately, there is a need for animal sanctuaries for many different animals.

Bengali is a male Siberian/Bengal Tiger, who lives at Big Cat Rescue in Tampa, Florida. He came to live at the sanctuary on December 5, 2000 when the circus who had him performing retired him at the age of five. To read more about Bengali visit http://bigcatrescue.org/bengali/.

An animal sanctuary makes a promise to provide shelter and care for animals that have been abused, **neglected**, or abandoned. It is a stable home for all kinds of animals. There are regulations and requirements on how to care for the animals. Any sanctuary that chooses to **exhibit** animals to the public participates in yearly inspections to ensure animals are cared for properly.

Some sanctuaries will allow visitors to view the less threatening animals up close, but the more threatening animals are sometimes off limits.

The Animal Sanctuary Association, started in 1998, works to help find homes for rescued animals. They also monitor the activities of active sanctuaries and review applications of new groups to ensure that a high standard of care is met by all of its members.

Chapter 3
Care and Comfort

There are many factors to consider when caring for wild animals. Caretakers feed animals on a regular schedule and provide them food that is close to or the same as what they might eat in the wild. Workers clean the **enclosures** regularly to keep animals in good health. Medical

A volunteer at Big Cat Rescue uses a special tool for operant conditioning training with Alex the cat. This trains the cat to do different behaviors so the vet can examine him.

staff monitors the health of the animals closely. Animals have opportunities for play and to participate in activities to ensure they remain fit. Animals that come to the facility with health concerns or injuries are **rehabilitated** and cared for by humans who try to earn their trust.

BIG CAT RESCUE

Big Cat Rescue is a non-profit educational sanctuary located in Tampa, Florida. Carole Baskin initially became involved with big cats when she wanted to purchase a pet bobcat. Through lots of experiences, she realized that big cats were not meant to be pets or performers and founded Big Cat Rescue.

Today, Big Cat Rescue houses 100 cats from 12 different species. It's the most species of any big cat sanctuary in the world. Eighty percent of the cats were once pets.

In addition to feeding and housing the cats, it's important to provide stimulation for the cats. Willow Hetch, is in charge of big cat enrichment activities. Some of the things they do for the cats are:

- *Give them seasonal things like pumpkins, Christmas trees, and paper mache Easter eggs.*
- *Make "bloodcicles" for them in the summer.*
- *Give them cardboard boxes and scented toilet paper rolls.*
- *Let them paint with non-toxic paints.*
- *Give them catnip.*

To learn more about Big Cat Rescue, you can visit them at www.bigcatrescue.org.

Sabre is a male leopard. He has been living at Big Cat Rescue since July 20, 1995 when he was abandoned by his owner. For an old cat, Sabre loves to jump and run around his cat-a-tat! To learn more about Sabre visit http://bigcatrescue.org/sabre-2/.

Is a zoo the same thing as a sanctuary? Although they seem the same, they have different qualities. A zoo is a place created to show animals to the public. They sometimes monitor animals to collect information about a **species** or scientists will conduct research experiments to learn more about a particular animal. Animals in zoos tend to be popular animals, the kind that make people curious and want to visit. Unlike an animal sanctuary, zoo animals can be bought, sold, borrowed, or loaned to other facilities. Some zoos also run breeding programs.

Zoos are popular destinations for people to learn about animals they would normally never be able to see without traveling to exotic locations.

The Woodstock Sanctuary in New York cares for rescued farm animals. Chickens, goats, rabbits, cows, sheep, and pigs all share this protected home. This special sanctuary believes in kindness and respect for all animals. They believe we should share the Earth with animals instead of using animals for food.

Chapter 4

Inform and Educate

Sanctuaries do more than provide a safe home. Not only do they provide care for the animals, but many sanctuaries also provide education and information to the public. What do people need to know? Unusual or wild **carnivorous** animals do not make good pets. Some people think it is exciting or fun to have a tiger or lion as a pet. Unfortunately, a family or community could be put at risk by keeping an animal that can be dangerous to keep as a pet.

FURRY FACT

A group called Born Free USA started tracking incidents involving wild animals kept as pets in 1990. Since they began collecting data, they found at least 2,094 incidents, 83 of them resulting in death. They believe that if all incidents were properly reported, that number would be much higher.

Does Your State Allow Wild Animals to be Owned as Pets?

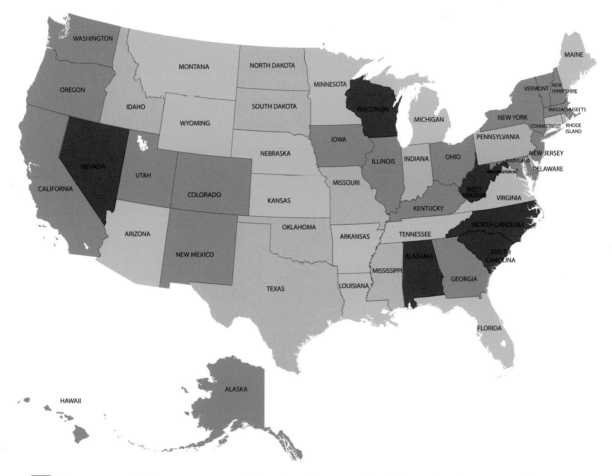

■ Bans most dangerous wild animals as pets (big cats, bears, wolves, primates, some reptiles)

■ Bans some species of dangerous wild animals as pets but allows others

■ Does not ban dangerous wild animals as pets but requires permits for some species

■ Does not regulate or restrict dangerous wild animals at all

Source: Humanesociety.org

Sanctuaries want people to know that large cats and wild animals are not entertainment. Many people want these animals to use their bodies and skins to make products. Sanctuaries hope people recognize that animals are living creatures, not products. They want to increase awareness about the nature of these animals and change how people think about them.

How Can You Help?

Use your voice to share what you know about animals taken from the wild. Explain what animals make good pets and let others know about sanctuaries.

Create a video, poster or add to a blog to spread the word.

Become an advocate. Help stop abuse and support laws that protect animals.

Donate your time or collect supplies to help a sanctuary in your area.

Hold a fundraiser to collect money for a local animal sanctuary.

Have your class contact a local sanctuary and find out what special things they need for the animals on holidays. Then, have everyone bring one item from the list to donate.

Glossary

carnivorous (kar-NIV-ur-uhss): eating meat

enclosures (en-KLOH-zhurz): areas closed in by a fence, wall, or other object

exhibit (eg-ZIB-it): to show something to the public

exotic (eg-ZOT-ik): strange and fascinating

habitat (HAB-uh-tat): the natural place where a plant or animal lives

neglected (ni-GLEKT-ed): not looked after properly, to fail to take care of someone or something

protected (pruh-TEKT-id): guarded, kept safe from injury, attack, or harm

rehabilitated (re-huh-BIL-uh-tayt-ed): restored to a condition of good health

sanctuary (SANGK-choo-er-ee): a natural area where animals are provided safety and protection

species (SPEE-sheez): a specific type or group of animals with shared characteristics

unique (yoo-NEEK): one of a kind, unusual

Index

Show What You Know

1. What is the difference between a zoo and a sanctuary?
2. How does a sanctuary provide care for its animals?
3. Why is there a need for animal sanctuaries?
4. What is a poacher? How does a poacher impact an animal population?
5. What can you do to help?

Websites to Visit

http://www.earthskids.com/help_animals.htm

http://www.paws.org/kids/learn/wild-animals/

http://www.bornfreeusa.org/database/index_exo_incidents.php

About the Author

Kelli Hicks is a teacher and author who calls her home in Tampa, Florida her sanctuary. She lives with her husband, daughter, son and two dogs. She enjoys curling up with a good book, watching her kids run wild on the soccer field, and letting her dogs take her for a walk.

Meet The Author!
www.meetREMauthors.com

© 2015 Rourke Educational Media

www.rourkeeducationalmedia.com

PHOTO CREDITS: Cover © Johan Swanepoel, kali9, SpeedPhoto; title page © Rich Carey; page 4 © Maggy Meyer; page 6 © Slava Samusevich; page 7 © Nico Smit, joruba; page 8 © Maria Feklistova; page 9 © Big Cat Rescue, Tampa, FL.; page 10 © Louie Schoeman; page 11 © WoodenDinosaur; page 12, 13 © Big Cat Rescue, Tampa, FL.; page 14 © Thitsan; page 15 © Maurice van der Velden; page 17 © Natasha Tatarin; page 19 © Bildagentur Zoonar GmbH; page 20 © Jodi Jacobson; page 21 © rmarmion, mangostock

Edited by: Luana Mitten

Cover and Interior design by: Jen Thomas

Library of Congress PCN Data

Animal Sanctuaries/Kelli Hicks
(Animal Matters)
 ISBN 978-1-63430-066-7 (hard cover)
 ISBN 978-1-63430-096-4 (soft cover)
 ISBN 978-1-63430-122-0 (e-Book)
Library of Congress Control Number: 2014953370

Printed in the United States of America, North Mankato, Minnesota

Also Available as: